Sing at First Sight

Foundations in Choral Sight-Singing

Level 1

Andy Beck

Karen Farnum Surmani

Brian Lewis

Alfred

Table of Contents

> *Beat, Rhythm, Notes, Rests, Staff, Treble Clef, Lines and Spaces, Ledger Lines, Flat, Sharp, Key Signature, Time Signature, Bar Lines, Measures, Double Bar Lines*

> *$\frac{4}{4}$ Time, Major Scale, C Major and F Major, Essential Exercise*

Unit 1

> *Repeat Sign, 1st and 2nd Endings, G Major and D Major, Essential Exercise*

Unit 2

> *Dynamic Signs ($\boldsymbol{pp}$, $\boldsymbol{p}$, $\boldsymbol{mp}$, $\boldsymbol{mf}$, $\boldsymbol{f}$, $\boldsymbol{ff}$), Crescendo, Decrescendo, B♭ Major and E♭ Major, Essential Exercise*

Unit 3

Unit 4

Unit 5

Unit 6

How to Use This Book

Each unit is preceded by a **Getting Ready** page, which introduces new musical concepts. Concepts are discussed in detail at the beginning of each lesson, so students are fully prepared for the exercises that follow. General musicianship, concentrating on topics such as dynamics, key signatures and tempo markings, is the focus of this section, while pitch and rhythm exercises are reserved for unit lessons.

An **Essential Exercise** is included in every **Getting Ready** section to prepare students for subsequent units. These exercises may be read or taught by rote and used for warm-up or review during each rehearsal. In addition, they provide the opportunity for students to practice new concepts before reading the corresponding notation.

Rhythm Exercises at the beginning of each lesson are designed to be spoken, clapped, tapped, or sung on a pitch.

Pitch Exercises are sequentially designed to challenge, yet nurture beginning sight-singers. There are many excellent techniques that work well with sight-singing. It is recommended that students sing the exercises in this book using solfège syllables, numbers, or note names to help establish a tonal base. However, it is not the intention of the authors to require the use of any single methodology, but rather to provide tools to allow teachers to make instructional choices that fit their own personal teaching style.

Challenge Exercises are sight-singing exercises that are a little more difficult. In addition to regular sight-singing practice, challenge exercises may be used for exams, friendly classroom competitions, or extra credit work.

An excerpt selected from Alfred Publishing's award-winning **Choral Designs** is included at the end of each unit and used to reinforce concepts that have been introduced. Although they are not intended for concert performance, these songs can be used in the classroom to assess progress.

Review pages at the end of each unit contain the following sections:

1. **Scavenger Hunt**
   Students identify concepts in the performance excerpt.

2. **Find the Wrong Note**
   The teacher plays a written musical example with an intentional wrong note or rhythm for the students to identify.

3. **Name That Tune**
   Students recognize familiar tunes by sight and develop their inner-hearing skills using an enjoyable game format.

4. **Evaluate Your Performance**
   Guided questions to help singers self-evaluate.

Two full-length **Performance Pieces** are included at the end of the book as an extension of the learning process. Once students complete the book, they will be able to sight-read and perform these selections under the guidance of their teacher.

The Importance of Sight-Singing

Sight-singing can be defined as the ability to accurately read and sing the pitches, rhythms, and words of a musical piece at first sight. Achieving competent sight-singing skills is a component of becoming a complete musician. Research has shown that regular sight-singing practice, for even small amounts of time, will improve skills in all areas of musicianship.

Singing Posture

Correct body alignment is very important for singers. Good posture makes managing the breath easier, which makes it easier to produce beautiful singing tones. Incorrect posture can induce physical tension and lead to vocal strain.

A singer's posture is flexible but stable, allowing the vocal mechanism to function freely.

When standing, the feet are planted firmly on the floor, approximately shoulder-width apart. Knees are relaxed, never locked. The spine is as straight as possible, but not rigid. Shoulders are down and back, but relaxed. The chest is open to allow for full expansion of the lungs. The arms are loose and relaxed.

When sitting, balance at the front of the chair with feet flat on the floor. The back should be straight, not touching the back of the chair, as if standing from the hips up.

Breathing

Proper breathing is essential to the singing process because the exhaled breath works with the vocal cords to create the singing tone. As a breath is inhaled in a relaxed manner, shoulders and chest also remain relaxed. Correct breathing utilizes the muscles in the lower abdominal region, the *diaphragm*, and allows the voice to gain its strength, agility, and finesse from this area, while avoiding any tension in the throat.

Breathing exercises:

1. To experience natural breathing, lie flat on your back and quietly observe your breathing. You will naturally breathe deeply and easily. Try to maintain this ease when you stand.

2. Hold the palm of your hand about 12 inches in front of your mouth. Sip the air in and expel it onto your palm in a slow, steady stream for as long as possible.

Curwen Hand Signs

Curwen Hand Signs were developed by the British music educator John Curwen in the nineteenth century. Each hand position represents a scale tone. Not only are the shapes of these signs important, but the level of the hand showing the sign should gradually raise or lower as the notes go up or down. Encouraging students to use Curwen Hand Signs can promote more tuneful singing as it provides a heightened awareness of a tone's relationship and proximity to the home tone, *Do.*

Ti

La

Sol

Fa

Mi

Re

Do

Before You Begin

Here are some music fundamentals you will need in order to *Sing at First Sight*. This section may be used either as a review or as introductory material. Teachers are encouraged to adapt or supplement these materials as determined by the needs of your students.

The *beat* is a steady pulse within music.

Rhythm is the organization of music in time using long and short note values.

Music *notes* are symbols that represent musical sounds (pitch and duration). Most notes are made up of an oval-shaped notehead and a stem. Stems extend upward on the right side of the notehead or downward on the left side of the notehead. Noteheads may be hollow or filled in.

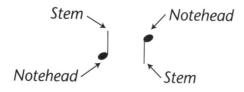

Symbols that represent periods of silence in music are called *rests*. During rests, the beat continues in the music, but the sound does not. Durations of rests are equal to the values of the equivalent note symbols.

The musical *staff* is made of five horizontal lines and four spaces on which notes are placed.

The *treble clef* is used for notes in higher pitch ranges.

Musical notes are named in a repeating fashion utilizing the first seven letters of the alphabet (A to G). In the treble clef, the notes placed on the lines are, from bottom to top, E G B D F. The saying "Every Good Boy Does Fine" is commonly used to remember the names of these notes. The names of the notes in the spaces spell out F A C E.

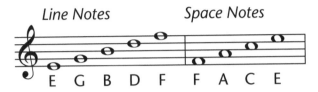

The treble clef is also called the *G clef*. Notice how the widest part of its curve circles the second staff line, the note G.

Ledger lines are short lines that are added to extend the range of the staff when notes are too low or too high to be written on the staff.

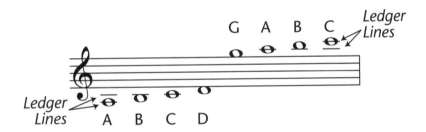

In Western music, a half step is the smallest distance between two notes. Two half steps equal one whole step. This can easily be shown on the piano keyboard.

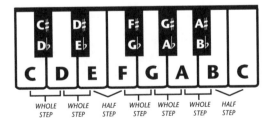

A *flat* sign ♭ lowers the pitch by one half step.

A *sharp* sign ♯ raises the pitch by one half step.

The *key signature* is a group of sharps or flats appearing at the beginning of a staff to establish the *key* (or location of *Do*). It indicates the notes that will be sharped or flatted each time they appear.

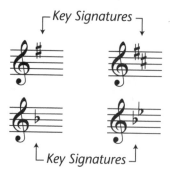

The *time signature*, or *meter*, of a musical piece is represented by the stacked numbers after the clef sign.

The top number indicates the number of beats in each measure. The bottom number indicates which type of note receives one beat.

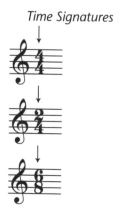

The vertical lines dividing the staff into sections are called *bar lines*. The areas between the bar lines are called *measures*.

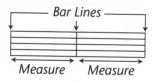

A *double bar line* consists of two vertical lines through the staff, signifying the end of a section, movement, or piece.

Getting Ready for Unit 1

■ In $\frac{4}{4}$ time there are four beats in each measure and the quarter note receives one beat.

1   2   3   4

■ The *major scale* is comprised of eight consecutive tones from *Do* to *Do* (or 1 to 8).

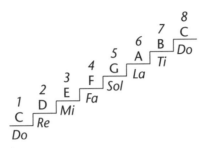

■ The key signature of *C major* has no sharps or flats.

Do   Re   Mi   Fa   Sol   La   Ti   Do
C   D   E   F   G   A   B   C

1   2   3   4   5   6   7   8

■ The key signature of *F major* has one flat: on the B line.

Do   Re   Mi   Fa   Sol   La   Ti   Do
F   G   A   B♭   C   D   E   F

1   2   3   4   5   6   7   8

Hint

For key signatures with flats, the last flat (the one farthest to the right) is *Fa,* the fourth note of the scale.

Essential Exercise

Sing this exercise as preparation for sight-singing in Unit 1.

Do	Re	Mi	Fa	Sol	La	Ti	Do	Ti	La	Sol	Fa	Mi	Re	Do
1	2	3	4	5	6	7	8	7	6	5	4	3	2	1

Lesson 1

■ A *quarter note* ♩ is equal to one beat. Say "ta" to count a quarter note.

ta ta ta ta
1 2 3 4

■ A *quarter rest* 𝄽 is equal to one beat of silence. Think "ta" to count a quarter rest.

ta ta ta ta
1 2 3 4

■ *Do* is the first note or home tone of the scale.

Key of C

Do

■ *Re* is the second note of the scale.

Key of C

Re

Rhythm Exercises

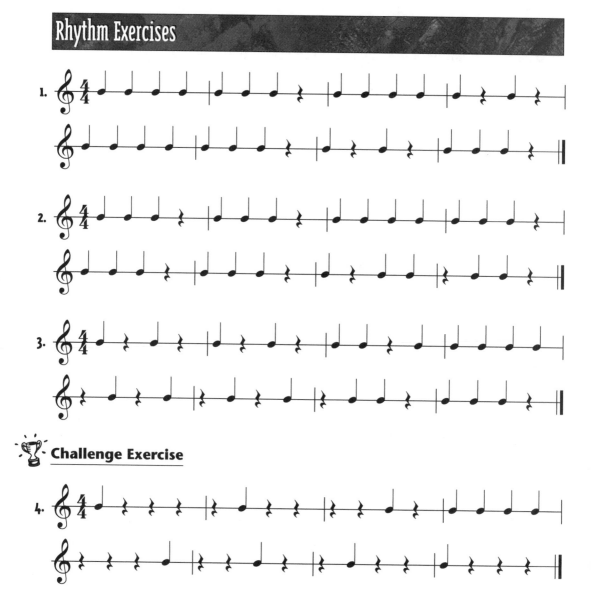

1.

2.

3.

🏆 Challenge Exercise

4.

Pitch Exercises

Hint

Do can move. Notice the key signature. The next exercise is in the key of F.
Do is now in the first space.

Lesson 2

■ A *half note* 𝅗𝅥 is equal to two beats.
Say "ta-ah" to count a half note.

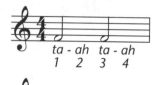

ta - ah ta - ah
1   2   3   4

■ A *half rest* ▬ is equal to two beats of silence.
Think "ta-ah" to count a half rest.

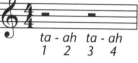

ta - ah ta - ah
1   2   3   4

■ *Mi* is the third note of the scale.

Key of C

Mi

■ *Fa* is the fourth note of the scale.

Key of C

Fa

Rhythm Exercises

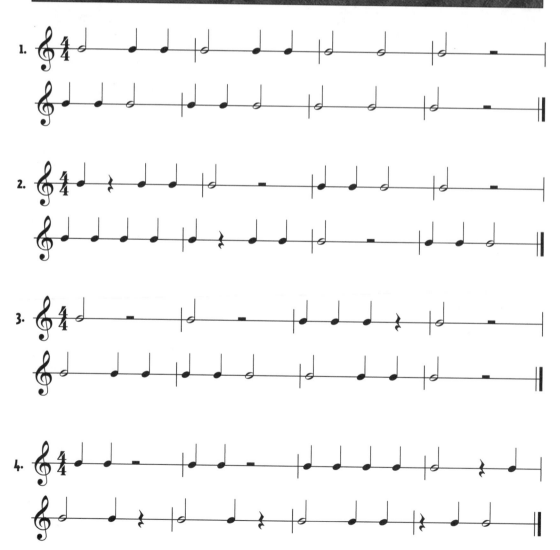

Pitch Exercises

Hint

It may be helpful to rehearse the rhythm first, before singing the pitches.

Challenge Exercise

UNIT 1

Lesson 3

■ A *whole note* o is equal to four beats.
Say "ta-ah-ah-ah" to count a whole note.

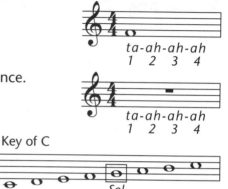

ta-ah-ah-ah
1 2 3 4

■ A *whole rest* ▬ is equal to four beats of silence.
Think "ta-ah-ah-ah" to count a whole rest.

ta-ah-ah-ah
1 2 3 4

■ *Sol* is the fifth note of the scale.

Key of C
Sol

■ *La* is the sixth note of the scale.

Key of C
La

Rhythm Exercises

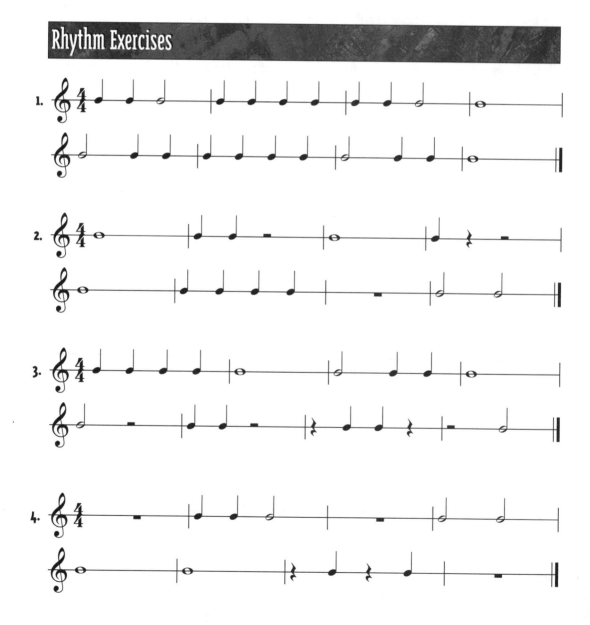

Pitch Exercises

Hint

Remember to sit or stand tall.

Challenge Exercise

This tune can be performed as a round.

*Part 2 begins when Part 1 gets to the third measure.

UNIT 1

Lesson 4

- An *eighth note* ♪ is equal to one-half beat. Say "ti" to count an eighth note.

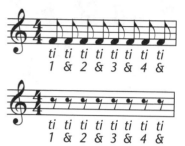

ti ti ti ti ti ti ti ti
1 & 2 & 3 & 4 &

- An *eighth rest* ↱ is equal to one-half beat of silence. Think "ti" to count an eighth rest.

ti ti ti ti ti ti ti ti
1 & 2 & 3 & 4 &

- An eighth note may be notated in the following ways:

1. with a flag   *2. beamed in pairs*   *3. beamed in threes*   *4. beamed in fours*

- *Ti* is the seventh note of the scale.

Key of C

Ti

- *High Do* is the eighth note of the scale.

Key of C

High Do

Rhythm Exercises

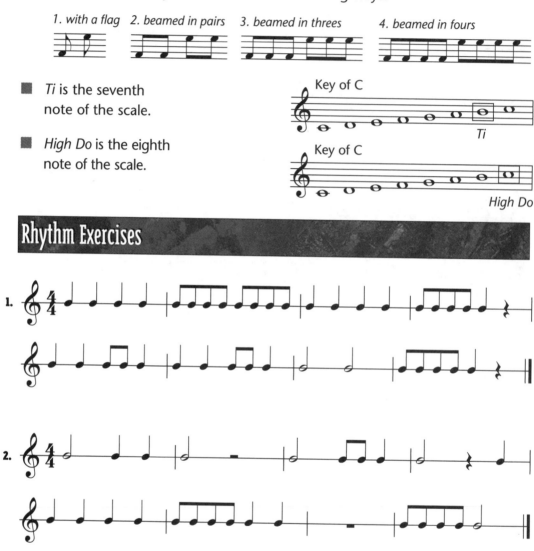

1.

2.

:🔅: **Hint**

Accuracy is more important than speed. Take it slow.

3.

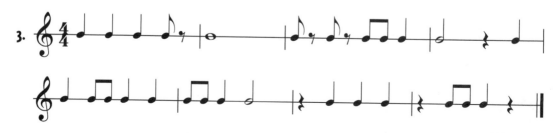

Pitch Exercises

4.

Hint

Remember to take a full, relaxed breath and avoid tension in the throat as you sing.

5.

6.

7.

8.

Challenge Exercise

9.

Choral Designs

This is the first song in the book with piano accompaniment.

Notice that the piano part is always printed under the vocal part.

Separating the elements of music is an effective way to learn a piece.

■ First, practice the rhythms.

■ Next, sing the pitches.

■ Finally, add the words.

Goals for "Song of Joy"

■ Find the starting vocal pitch in the piano part.

■ Sing with expression.

Song of Joy

excerpt adapted from Alfred's Choral Designs series

Words and Music by
JAY ALTHOUSE

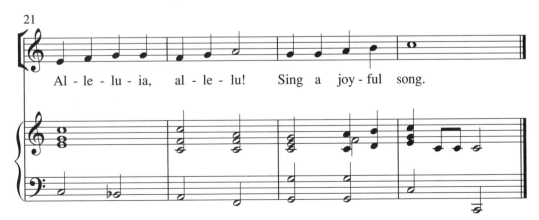

Available for 2-part voices, Level One (5797).

UNIT 1

Unit 1 Review

Scavenger Hunt

Find the following musical items in the excerpt "Song of Joy."

a half note

Do

a half rest

a whole note

a whole rest

Sol

Ti

a pair of eighth notes

Find the Wrong Note

Your teacher will sing or play the following examples with one or more intentional errors. Identify the notes or rhythms that are incorrectly performed.

Evaluating Your Performance

■ Were you able to correctly perform the pitches and rhythms in Unit 1?

■ How can you improve your performance?
(Posture, pitch, rhythm, breathing?)

■ Did you feel confident about your performance of "Song of Joy?"

Getting Ready for Unit 2

■ A *repeat sign*  indicates that a section of music is to be repeated.

■ At a repeat sign, go back to the beginning of the song. Sometimes, repeat signs appear in pairs within the music. The first repeat sign will have the two dots placed after the double bar. When this occurs, return to the first repeat sign at the beginning of the section.

Go back and repeat.

■ *1st* and *2nd endings* indicate to play or sing through the 1st ending to the repeat sign, then go back to the beginning. On the repeat, skip the 1st ending and sing the 2nd ending.

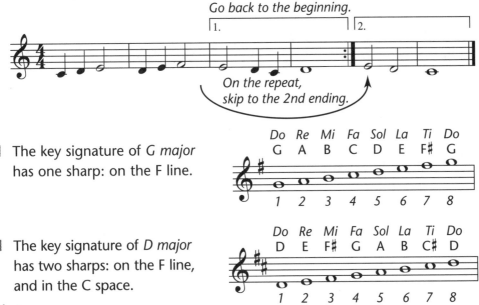

Go back to the beginning.

On the repeat, skip to the 2nd ending.

■ The key signature of *G major* has one sharp: on the F line.

	Do	Re	Mi	Fa	Sol	La	Ti	Do
	G	A	B	C	D	E	F♯	G
	1	2	3	4	5	6	7	8

■ The key signature of *D major* has two sharps: on the F line, and in the C space.

	Do	Re	Mi	Fa	Sol	La	Ti	Do
	D	E	F♯	G	A	B	C♯	D
	1	2	3	4	5	6	7	8

Hint

For key signatures with sharps, the last sharp
(the one farthest to the right) is *Ti*, the seventh note of the scale.

Essential Exercise

Sing this exercise as preparation for sight-singing in Unit 2.

Do	Mi	Re	Fa	Mi	Sol	Fa	La	Sol	Ti	La	Do	Ti	Re	Do
1	3	2	4	3	5	4	6	5	7	6	8	7	2	8

Do	La	Ti	Sol	La	Fa	Sol	Mi	Fa	Re	Mi	Do	Re	Ti	Do
8	6	7	5	6	4	5	3	4	2	3	1	2	7	1

Lesson 5

UNIT 2

A *tie* is a curved line that joins two notes of the same pitch to make one long sound. The tied note's value is added to the value of the first note.

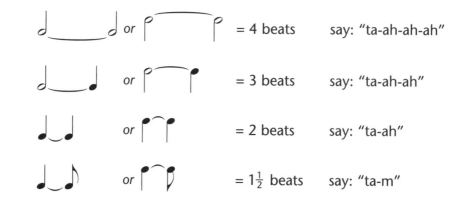

= 4 beats	say: "ta-ah-ah-ah"
= 3 beats	say: "ta-ah-ah"
= 2 beats	say: "ta-ah"
= $1\frac{1}{2}$ beats	say: "ta-m"

Rhythm Exercises

Hint

Ties can cross bar lines.

Challenge Exercise

Pitch Exercises

Challenge Exercise

Lesson 6

■ A *dot* after a note increases the note's duration by half the original value.

■ A *dotted half note* 𝅗𝅥· is equal to three beats. Say "ta-ah-ah" to count a dotted half note.

■ *Low Ti* is one note below *Do*.

■ *High Re* is one note above *High Do*.

Rhythm Exercises

Pitch Exercises

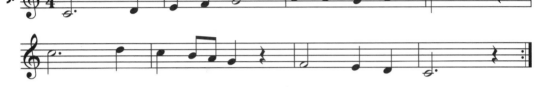

Hint
Count carefully.

Lesson 7

UNIT 2

■ A *dotted quarter note* ♩· is equal to one and one-half beats. Say "ta-m" to count a dotted quarter note.

ta-m ta-m
1 & 2 & 3 & 4 &

■ Dotted quarter notes are often combined with eighth notes to create new rhythmic patterns. Two commonly used patterns are:

Say "ta-m-ti" to count dotted quarter-eighth note patterns.

ta-m- ti
1 & 2 &

Say "ti-ta-m" to count eighth-dotted quarter note patterns.

ti- ta - m
1 & 2 &

■ *Low La* is the scale tone two notes below *Do*.

Key of C

Low La

■ *Low Sol* is the scale tone three notes below *Do*.

Key of C

Low Sol

Rhythm Exercises

1.

2.

Challenge Exercise

3.

Pitch Exercises

4.

5.

6.

💡 **Hint**

Think the pitch before you sing.

7.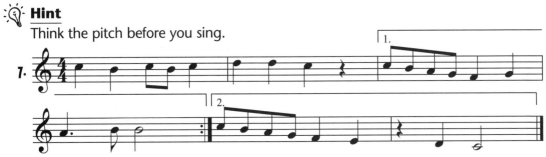

🏆 **Challenge Exercise**

After singing exercises 8 and 9 separately, they can be performed simultaneously!

8.

9.

Lesson 8

■ An *interval* is the distance in pitch from one note to another. The interval is counted from the lower note to the higher one, with the lower note counted as 1.

■ The interval of a *2nd* spans the distance of two notes. For example, from *Do* to *Re* or *Re* to *Mi*.

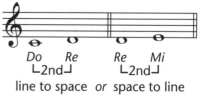

Do　　Re　　　Re　　Mi
└2nd┘　　　└2nd┘
line to space *or* space to line

■ The interval of a *3rd* spans the distance of three notes. For example, from *Do* to *Mi* or *Re* to *Fa*.

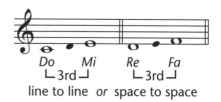

Do　　Mi　　Re　　Fa
└3rd┘　　　└3rd┘
line to line *or* space to space

Rhythm Exercises

Challenge Exercise

Pitch Exercises

This tune can be performed as a round. *Part 2 begins when Part 1 gets to the third measure.

Hint

Before you sing an exercise, take a moment of silent study to identify challenging intervals.

Challenge Exercise

After singing exercises 9 and 10 separately, they can be performed simultaneously!

Choral Designs

Goals for "Sleep, My Child"

- Navigate all repeat signs and endings successfully.
- Sing smoothly and expressively, as a lullaby.

Sleep, My Child

excerpt adapted from Alfred's Choral Designs series*

New Words by
MARY DONNELLY (ASCAP)

Arranged, with New Music by
GEORGE L.O. STRID (ASCAP)

Sleep, my child, and peace at-tend thee,
Guard - ian an - gels God will send thee,

all through the night.

May your dreams all come true while you are gent-ly sleep - ing.

When you are grown, you will find all the world is in your

21

keep - ing. I my lov - ing

25

vig - il keep - ing, all through the

1.

night.

2.

Yes, night.

decresc.

pp

* Available for 2-part voices, Level Two (21142). SoundTrax CD available (21143).

Unit 2 Review

Scavenger Hunt

Find the following musical items in the excerpt "Sleep, My Child."

a dotted half note	*two repeat signs*	*an interval of a 3rd*
an interval of a 2nd	*a 1st ending*	*Low Sol*
Low Ti	*Low La*	*the note B*

Find the Wrong Note

Your teacher will sing or play the following examples with one or more intentional errors. Identify the notes or rhythms that are incorrectly performed.

Name That Tune

Your teacher will sing or play the starting pitches of these familiar songs. Sing the songs in your head and identify the tunes.

Evaluating Your Performance

- Which intervals were difficult for you in "Sleep, My Child?"
- How can you improve your performance? (Posture, pitch, rhythm, breathing?)
- Were you able to convey the feeling of a lullaby when you sang "Sleep, My Child?"

Getting Ready for Unit 3

■ *Dynamic signs* indicate the volume, or how soft or loud the music should be sung. Most musical terms are written in Italian since Italian composers were among the first to write such instructions in their manuscripts.

Italian	Sign	English
pianissimo	***pp***	very soft
piano	***p***	soft
mezzo piano	***mp***	moderately soft
mezzo forte	***mf***	moderately loud
forte	***f***	loud
fortissimo	***ff***	very loud

crescendo or ***cresc.***
means gradually louder.

decrescendo or ***decresc.***
means gradually softer.

■ The key signature of *B♭ major* has two flats: on the B line, and in the E space.

■ The key signature of *E♭ major* has three flats: on the B line, in the E space, and in the A space.

Essential Exercise

Sing this exercise as preparation for sight-singing in Unit 3.

Lesson 9

- In $\frac{3}{4}$ *time* there are three beats in each measure and the quarter note receives one beat.

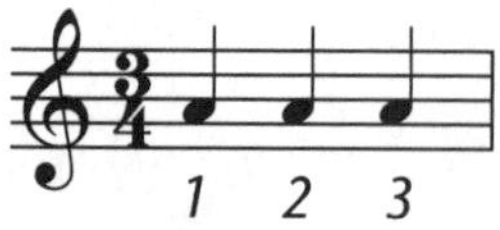

- In $\frac{2}{4}$ *time* there are two beats in each measure and the quarter note receives one beat.

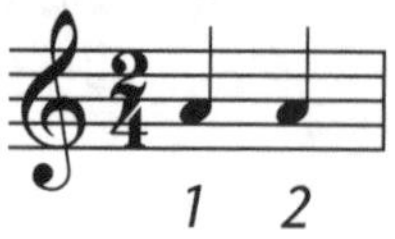

- A whole rest is used to indicate a complete measure of rest for all time signatures.

In $\frac{4}{4}$ time, a whole rest is equal to 4 beats of silence.

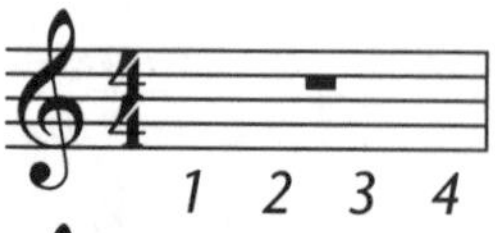

In $\frac{3}{4}$ time, a whole rest is equal to 3 beats of silence.

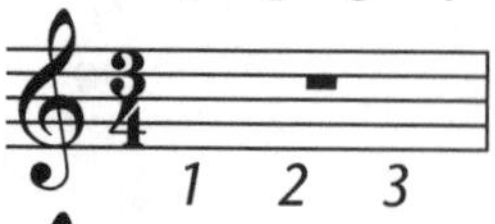

In $\frac{2}{4}$ time, a whole rest is equal to 2 beats of silence.

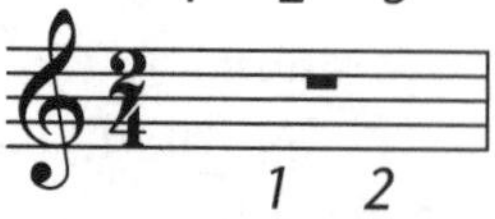

Rhythm Exercises

1.
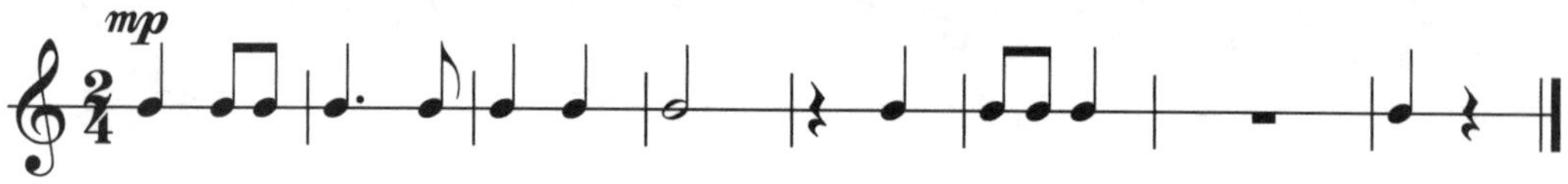

2.
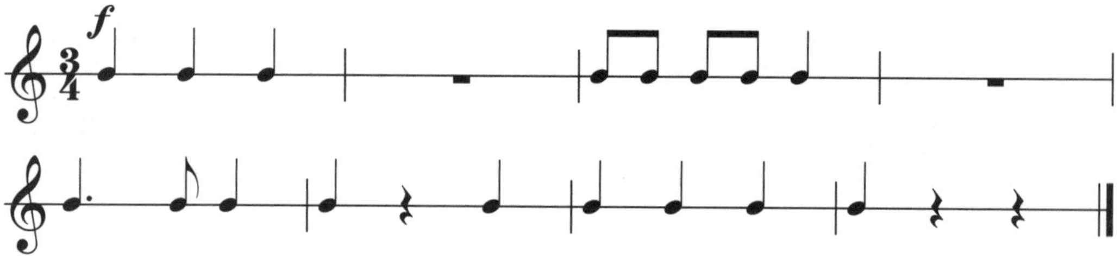

Hint

A *fermata* 𝄐 means to hold the note longer than its normal duration.

3.
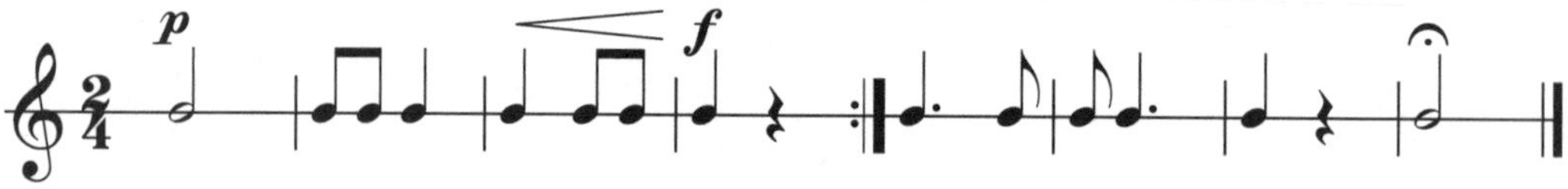

4.
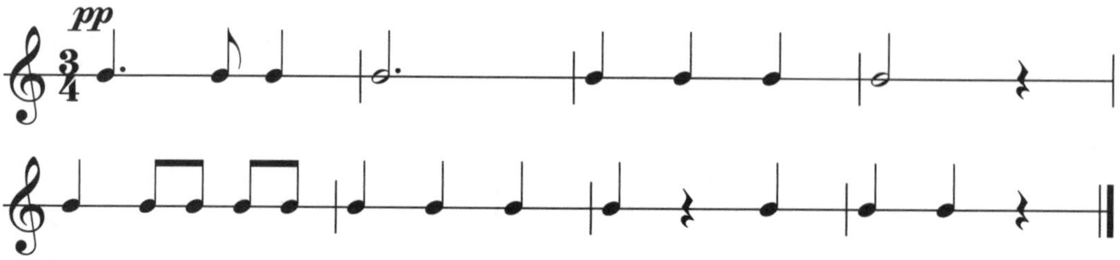

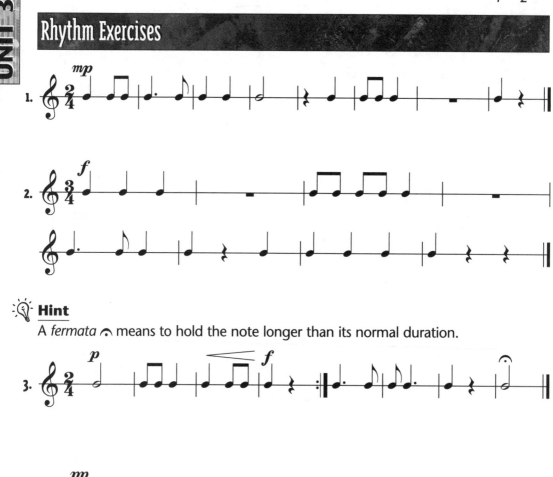

Pitch Exercises

Hint

Melodies can begin on any scale tone. To determine the first note, identify the key, find *Do*, and count up or down to find the starting syllable or number.

Hint

Look for patterns in the music.

Challenge Exercise

Lesson 10

■ The interval of an *8th* or *octave,* spans the distance of eight notes. For example, from *Do* to *High Do* or *Re* to *High Re.*

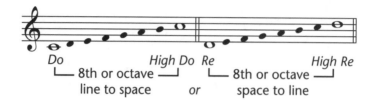

Do   High Do   Re   High Re
└── 8th or octave ──┘   └── 8th or octave ──┘
line to space   *or*   space to line

Rhythm Exercises

UNIT 3

☆ **Challenge Exercise**

Pitch Exercises

5.

6.

7.

💡 Hint

Singing softly requires extra breath support.

8.

9.

🏆 Challenge Exercise

10.

Lesson 11

■ Quarter notes are often combined with eighth notes to create a new rhythmic pattern. Say "syn-co-pa" to count eighth-quarter-eighth note combinations.

syn - co - pa   syn - co - pa
1   & 2 &   3   & 4 &

■ The interval of a *4th* spans the distance of four notes. For example, from *Do* to *Fa* or *Re* to *Sol*.

Do   Fa   Re   Sol
└── 4th ──┘   └── 4th ──┘
line to space   *or*   space to line

Rhythm Exercises

Hint

f–p means first time loud, second time soft.

Pitch Exercises

5.

6.

7.

8.

9.

🏆 Challenge Exercise

10.

Lesson 12

■ The interval of a *5th* spans the distance of five notes.
For example, from *Do* to *Sol* or *Re* to *La*.

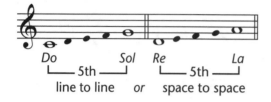

Do · · Sol Re · · · La
└── 5th ──┘ └── 5th ──┘
line to line   *or*   space to space

Rhythm Exercises

UNIT 3

🏆 **Challenge Exercise**

Pitch Exercises

5.

6.

7.

8.

💡 Hint

Before singing an exercise, take a moment of silent study to identify challenging rhythms.

9.

🏆 Challenge Exercise

10.

Choral Designs

UNIT 3

Goals for "Where Go the Boats"

- Sing long phrases, breathing only on rests.
- Be sure to sing with dynamic contrasts.

Where Go the Boats

excerpt adapted from Alfred's Choral Designs series*

Words from A Child's Garden of Verses
by **ROBERT LOUIS STEVENSON**

Music by
DAVE and JEAN PERRY (ASCAP)

Flowing (♩ = ca. 98)

PIANO — *mp*

5 VOICES — *mp*

Dark brown the riv-er,— Gold-en the sand. It

9

flows a-long for-ev-er, with trees on ei-ther hand.

13

Green leaves a-float-ing,— Cas-tles of foam,

From THREE POEMS, available for 2-part voices, Level Two (21648).

Unit 3 Review

Scavenger Hunt

Find the following musical items in the excerpt "Where Go the Boats."

a dynamic of *mf-mp*

a key signature of B♭

two decrescendos

a dotted quarter note

a tied note

an interval of a 4th

a single eighth note

a fermata

a melodic section that begins on a note other than *Do*

Find the Wrong Note

Your teacher will sing or play the following examples with one or more intentional errors. Identify the notes or rhythms that are incorrectly performed.

Name That Tune

Your teacher will sing or play the starting pitches of these familiar songs. Sing the songs in your head and identify the tunes.

Evaluating Your Performance

■ Which intervals were difficult for you in "Where Go the Boats?"

■ How can you improve your performance?
(Posture, pitch, rhythm, breathing?)

■ Were you able to sing the long phrases in "Where Go the Boats?"

UNIT 3

Getting Ready for Unit 4

■ The *bass clef* is the clef used for lower pitch ranges. 𝄢

■ In the bass clef, the notes placed on the lines are, from bottom to top, G B D F A. The saying "Good Boys Do Fine Always" is commonly used to remember the names of these notes. The names of the notes in the spaces are, A C E G. The saying "All Cows Eat Grass" is commonly used to remember the names of these notes.

Line Notes   Space Notes   Ledger Lines

G B D F A   A C E G   C D E F   B C D E

■ The bass clef is also called the *F clef*. Notice that the two dots are positioned around the fourth staff line, the note F.

■ ***D.C. (da capo) al Fine*** – go back to the beginning and sing to the end (***Fine***).

■ ***D.S. (dal segno) al Fine*** – go back to the sign 𝄋 and sing to the end (***Fine***).

■ ***D.C. al Coda*** – go back to the beginning and skip to the *coda* (an added ending) at the coda sign 𝄌.

■ ***D.S. al Coda*** – go back to the sign and skip to the coda at the coda sign.

■ The key signature of *A major* has three sharps: on the F line, in the C space, and in the G ledger space.

■ The key signature of *E major* has four sharps: on the F line, in the C space, in the G ledger space, and on the D line.

	Do	Re	Mi	Fa	Sol	La	Ti	Do
	A	B	C♯	D	E	F♯	G♯	A
	1	2	3	4	5	6	7	8

	Do	Re	Mi	Fa	Sol	La	Ti	Do
	E	F♯	G♯	A	B	C♯	D♯	E
	1	2	3	4	5	6	7	8

Essential Exercise

Sing this exercise as preparation for sight-singing in Unit 4.

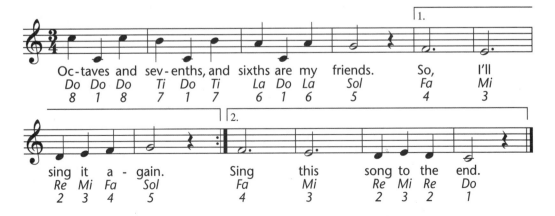

	Oc-taves	and	sev-enths,	and	sixths	are	my	friends.	So,	I'll
	Do	Do	Do	Ti	Do	Ti	La	Do La	Sol	Fa	Mi
	8	1	8	7	1	7	6	1 6	5	4	3

sing	it	a-	gain.	Sing	this	song	to	the	end.
Re	Mi	Fa	Sol	Fa	Mi	Re	Mi	Re	Do
2	3	4	5	4	3	2	3	2	1

Lesson 13

■ The interval of a *6th* spans the distance of six notes.
For example, from *Do* to *La* or *Re* to *Ti*.

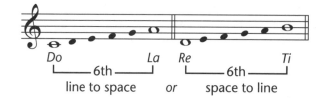

Rhythm Exercises

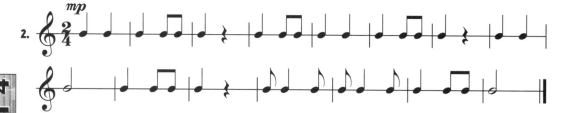

Pitch Exercises

UNIT 4

Hint

Use the proper amount of breath support to produce a full sound. Avoid vocal strain.

Challenge Exercise

Lesson 14

■ The interval of a *7th* spans the distance of seven notes.
For example, from *Do* to *Ti* or *Re* to *Do*.

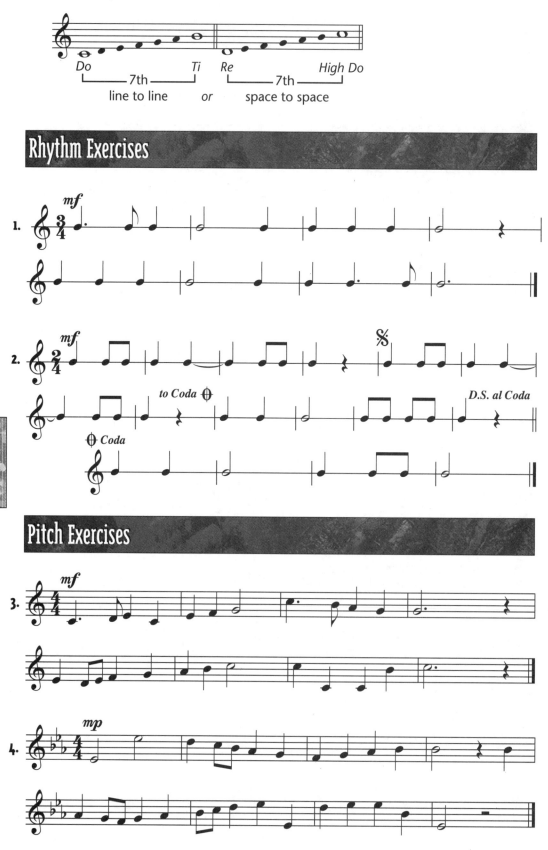

Rhythm Exercises

Pitch Exercises

Hint

Memorize the pitch of notes that reappear. Here, memorize *Do*.

Challenge Exercise

Lesson 15

■ The meter or time signature of music may change within a piece. When this occurs, the new time signature is placed at the beginning of a measure. The music that follows will be in the new meter.

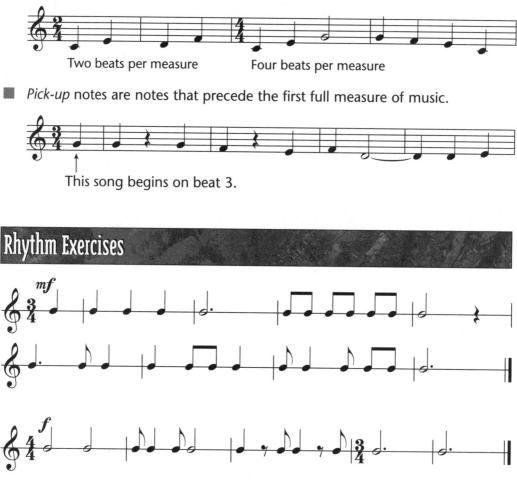

Two beats per measure   Four beats per measure

■ *Pick-up* notes are notes that precede the first full measure of music.

This song begins on beat 3.

Rhythm Exercises

1.

2.

Hint

Beat 1 of a measure is called the downbeat. Emphasize the downbeat when changing meters.

3.

4.

UNIT 4

Pitch Exercises

Challenge Exercise

Lesson 16

■ A *sixteenth note* ♪ is equal to one-quarter beat. Say "ti-ka" to count two sixteenth notes.

ti-ka ti-ka ti-ka ti-ka
1 e & a 2 e & a

Two sixteenth notes = one eighth note. ♫ = ♪

Four sixteenth notes = one quarter note. ♬ = ♩

■ A sixteenth note may be notated several ways, some of which are:

1. *with a flag*   2. *beamed in pairs*   3. *beamed in fours*

■ Sixteenth notes are often connected to eighth notes with a beam to create new rhythmic patterns. Two commonly used patterns are:

Say "ti-ka-ti" to count sixteenth-eighth note patterns.

ti-ka-ti
1 e & a

Say "ti-ti-ka" to count eighth-sixteenth note patterns.

ti - ti-ka
1 e & a

Rhythm Exercises

Pitch Exercises

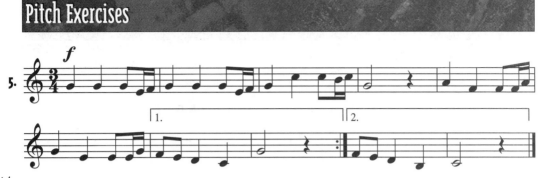

Hint

Do or *1* is the anchor tone. When singing a melody, always remember where *Do* is.

Challenge Exercise

This tune can be performed as a three-part round. Part 2 begins when Part 1 gets to the fifth measure, and Part 3 begins when Part 1 gets to the ninth measure.

Choral Designs

Goals for "La Música"

■ Practice the Spanish words, emphasizing the vowels.

■ Sing the intervals accurately, without scooping the pitch.

La Música

excerpt adapted from Alfred's Choral Designs series*

Words and Music by
JERRY ESTES

UNIT 4

Pronunciation & translation: *Lah moo-see-kah, moo-see-kah yeh-nah ehl koh-rah-sohn.*
(The music, music fills the heart.)

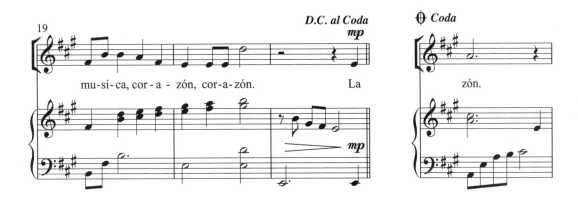

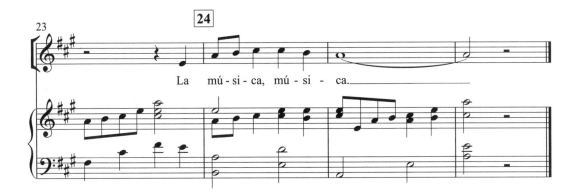

* From DOS CANCIÓNCITAS (Two Little Songs), available for 2-part voices, Level Two (20110).
  SoundTrax CD available (20111).

Unit 4 Review

Scavenger Hunt

Find the following musical items in the excerpt "La Música."

a coda	*a pickup note*	*two sets of double bar lines*
a pair of sixteenth notes	*a time signature*	*an interval of a 6th*
a crescendo	*an interval of a 7th*	*a tie*

Find the Wrong Note

Your teacher will sing or play the following examples with one or more intentional errors. Identify the notes or rhythms that are incorrectly performed.

Name That Tune

Your teacher will sing or play the starting pitches of these familiar songs. Sing the songs in your head and identify the tunes.

Evaluating Your Performance

- Which intervals were difficult for you in "La Música?"
- How can you improve your performance? (Posture, pitch, rhythm, breathing, dynamics?)
- Were you able to sing expressively in Spanish?

Getting Ready for Unit 5

- *Articulation marks* indicate how a note should be performed.

- A *slur* means to smoothly connect two or more notes of different pitches. This is called *legato* singing. For singers, a slur indicates to sing more than one pitch on a syllable of the text.

- A *staccato* mark means to sing the note short and detached.

- An *accent* mark means to sing the note stronger, with special emphasis.

- A *tenuto* mark means to sing a note with a slight stress. It can also mean to hold the note for its full value.

- The key signature of *A♭ major* has four flats: on the B line, in the E space, in the A space, and on the D line.

- The key signature of *D♭ major* has five flats: on the B line, in the E space, in the A space, on the D line, and on the G line.

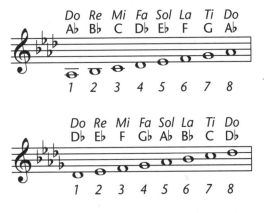

Essential Exercise

Sing this exercise as preparation for sight-singing in Unit 5. This tune can be performed as a three-part round. Part 2 begins when Part 1 gets to the fifth measure, and Part 3 begins when Part 1 gets to the ninth measure.

Traditional

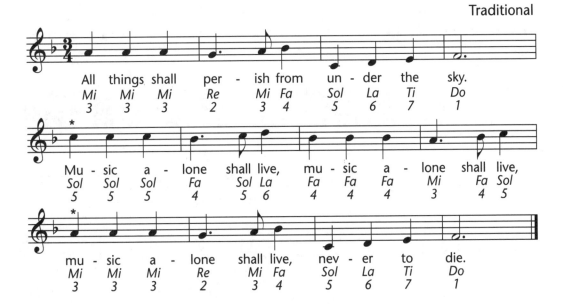

Lesson 17

■ In a *round* or *canon* two or more parts sing the same music at different times. The melody (tune) is sung by one group, followed by another group performing the same melody. Each entrance starts at a specified time.

■ When learning a canon, it is helpful to sing the music in unison (together) first before dividing into parts. Try this method with the examples in Lesson 17. Concentrate on hearing your part.

All of the exercises in this lesson can be performed in canon.
*Part 2 begins when Part 1 gets to the star *.*

Hint
Sing with confidence.

Challenge Exercise
This round is in 3 parts.

Challenge Exercise

W. A. Mozart
(1756–1791)

Lesson 18

- When two or more musical lines are performed simultaneously, they create *harmony*.

- When singing in two-part harmony:

One section sings this line ⟶

Another section sings this line ⟶

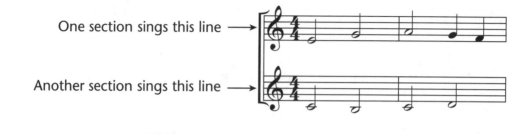

Rhythm Exercises

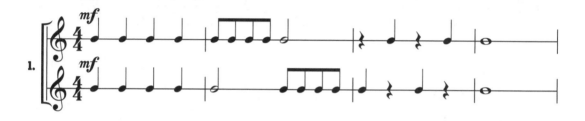

1.

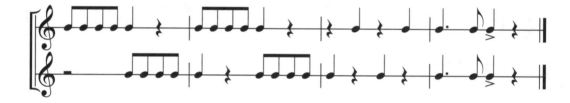

2.

Pitch Exercises

3.

UNIT 5

Hint

Be sure to keep your eyes on your own musical line.

Challenge Exercise

Lesson 19

- A *dotted eighth note* ♪. is equal to one-half plus one-quarter beat (or one eighth note plus one sixteenth). ♪. = ♪ + ♬

- Dotted eighth notes are often connected to sixteenth notes with a beam to create new rhythmic patterns. Two commonly used patterns incorporating dotted eighth and sixteenth notes are:

  Say "tim-ka" to count dotted eighth-sixteenth note patterns.

  tim - ka
  1 e & a

  Say "tik-um" to count sixteenth-dotted eighth note patterns.

  tik-um
  1 e & a

Rhythm Exercises

UNIT 5

🏆 **Challenge Exercise**

Pitch Exercises

Hint

A dot above or below a note means to sing it short and detached. A dot following a note makes it longer.

Challenge Exercise

Lesson 20

■ When three notes are grouped together with a figure "3" above or below the notes, the group is called a *triplet*. The three notes are sung in the time of two notes of the same value.

Say "tri - o - la" to count triplets.

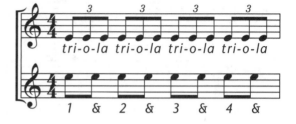

Rhythm Exercises

Pitch Exercises

Hint

Triplets should not be rushed.

Challenge Exercise

Choral Designs

Goals for "Frozen December"

■ Follow all changes of time signature.

■ Perform all articulation markings.

Frozen December

excerpt adapted from Alfred's Choral Designs series*

Catalan Carol

Arranged with English lyrics
by **JACKIE O'NEILL**

PART I

Cold De cem - ber's i - cy chill takes its leave of win - ter; Giv - ing

PART II

Cold De cem - ber's i - cy chill takes its leave of win - ter; Giv - ing

way to days of spring bring - ing buds so ten - der. In a

way to days of spring bring - ing buds so ten - der.

UNIT 5

Pronunciation: *doo-na raw, raw, raw, doo-na sah, sah, sah, doo-nah raw-sah bay-yah.*

** From TWO CATALAN CAROLS, available for S.A.T.B., Level Four (4787),
and 2-part voices, Level Two (4788).*

Unit 5 Review

Scavenger Hunt

Find the following musical items in the excerpt "Frozen December."

a slur	*a dotted eighth-sixteenth note pattern*	*a key signature*
staccato markings	*a tenuto line*	*an interval of a 5th*
a meter change	*an eighth rest*	*a crescendo*

Find the Wrong Note

Your teacher will sing or play the following examples with one or more intentional errors. Identify the notes or rhythms that are incorrectly performed.

Name That Tune

Your teacher will sing or play the starting pitches of these familiar songs. Sing the songs in your head and identify the tunes.

Evaluating Your Performance

- Did you observe the dynamic markings when you sang "Frozen December?"
- How can you improve your performance? (Posture, pitch, rhythm, breathing, articulation, dynamics?)
- What are the challenges of singing in harmony?

Getting Ready for Unit 6

■ *Tempo* is an Italian word meaning "rate of speed." Tempo marks indicate how fast or slow the music should be played. Tempo marks are written in Italian.

Italian	English
Largo	Very slow
Adagio	Slow
Andante	Moving along (walking speed)
Moderato	Moderately
Allegro	Fast
Presto	Very fast

■ The terms *ritardando* (***ritard.*** or ***rit.***) and *rallentando (**rall.**)* mean gradually slower.

■ *Accelerando* (***accel.***) means gradually faster.

■ *Molto*, meaning "very," can be combined with other terms, such as *molto accelerando*.

■ *Poco a poco*, meaning "little by little," can be combined with other terms, such as *ritardando poco a poco*.

■ The key signature of *B major* has five sharps: on the F line, in the C space, in the G ledger space, on the D line, and in the A space.

■ The key signature of *G♭ major* has six flats: on the B line, in the E space, in the A space, on the D line, on the G line, and in the C space.

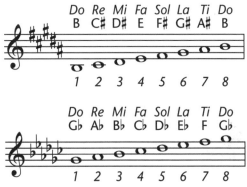

Essential Exercise

Sing this exercise as preparation for sight-singing in Unit 6.

Lesson 21

■ In $\frac{2}{2}$ *time* there are two beats in each measure and the half note receives one beat. This time signature is also called *cut time*.

Cut time can be abbreviated on the staff like this:

Rhythm Exercises

Pitch Exercises

4.

Hint

Find shared notes between parts and use them for tuning.

5.

Challenge Exercise

6.

Lesson 22

■ In $\frac{6}{8}$ *time* there are six beats in each measure and the eighth note receives one beat. Beats 1 and 4 are strong beats. At fast tempos, each $\frac{6}{8}$ measure can be counted in 2.

■ In $\frac{9}{8}$ *time* there are nine beats in each measure and the eighth note receives one beat. Beats 1, 4, and 7 are strong beats. At fast tempos, each $\frac{9}{8}$ measure can be counted in 3.

■ In both $\frac{6}{8}$ and $\frac{9}{8}$ time:

slow tempos	fast tempos
♪ or 𝄾 = 1 beat	♪ or 𝄾 = $\frac{1}{3}$ beat
♩ or 𝄾 = 2 beats	♩ or 𝄾 = $\frac{2}{3}$ beat
♩. or 𝄾. = 3 beats	♩. or 𝄾. = 1 beat

Rhythm Exercises

UNIT 6

Pitch Exercises

5.

Hint

In $\frac{6}{8}$ and $\frac{9}{8}$, emphasize the first note of the three-eighth-note patterns.

6.

 **Challenge Exercise**

7.

Lesson 23

When singing in three-part harmony:

One section sings this line →

Another section sings this line →

The third section sings this line →

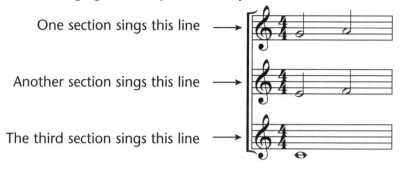

Rhythm Exercises

Pitch Exercises

💡 Hint

Rallentando and *Ritardando* markings are placed only above the top line of music.
Watch for ***rall.*** and ***rit.*** carefully.

💡 Hint

Listen to other sections and carefully tune the harmony.

🏆 Challenge Exercise

Lesson 24

When singing in three-part harmony:

One section sings this line →

Another section sings this line →

The third section sings this line →

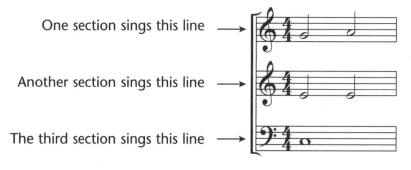

Rhythm Exercises

Moderato

1.

Adagio

2.

Pitch Exercises

Moderato

3.

UNIT 6

:💡: **Hint**

To stay in tune, sing each note in the center of the pitch.

Choral Designs

Goals for "Alleluia Madrigal"

■ Maintain a steady tempo throughout this excerpt. (Don't rush.)

■ Let your singing convey the joyful quality of this piece.

Alleluia Madrigal

excerpt adapted from Alfred's Choral Designs series*

Words and Music by
DONALD MOORE (ASCAP)

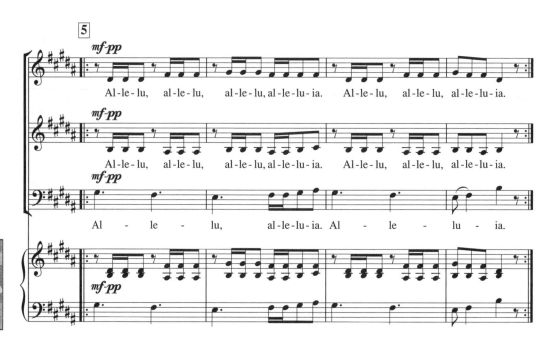

* Available for S.A.T.B., Level Four (21698), 3-part mixed, Level Three (21699),
and S.S.A., Level Three (21700).

Unit 6 Review

Scavenger Hunt

Find the following musical items in the excerpt "Alleluia Madrigal."

a fortissimo	*a slur*	*a key signature*
a ritard	*the note E in bass and treble clef*	*a tempo marking*
three repeat signs	*a fermata*	*an eighth rest*

Find the Wrong Note

Your teacher will sing or play the following examples with one or more intentional errors. Identify the notes or rhythms that are incorrectly performed.

Name That Tune

Your teacher will sing or play the starting pitches of these familiar songs. Sing the songs in your head and identify the tunes.

Evaluating Your Performance

- ■ Were you able to correctly sing the rhythms in "Alleluia Madrigal?"
- ■ How can you improve your performance?
  (Posture, pitch, rhythm, breathing, dynamics?)
- ■ What area of your performance has improved the most since beginning this book?

Sing Alleluia, Allelu!

from Alfred's Choral Designs series*

Words and Music by
ANDY BECK

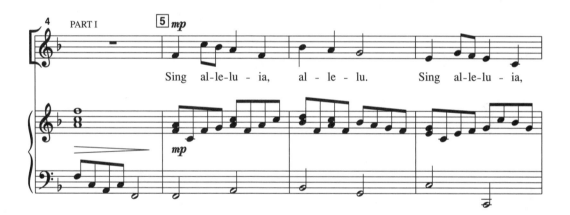

* *Available for 2-part voices with optional bell part, Level One (22979). SoundTrax CD available (22980).*

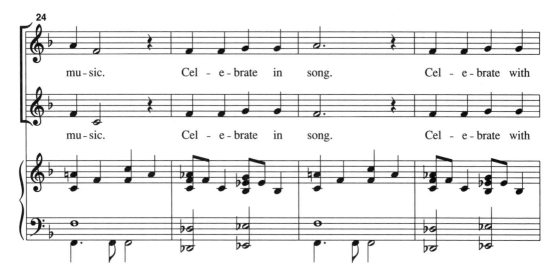

al - le - lu. Sing al-le-lu - ia.

lu - ia, ___ sing al-le-lu - ia, sing al-le-lu.

Cel - e-brate with

Cel - e-brate with

cym-bals. Make a joy-ful sound. Cel - e-brate with

cym-bals. Make a joy-ful sound. Cel - e-brate with

I Am a Small Part of the World

from Alfred's Choral Designs series*

Words and Music by
SALLY K. ALBRECHT
and **JAY ALTHOUSE**

* Available for S.A.T.B., Level Four (4742), 3-part mixed voices, Level Three (4743),
2-part voices, Level Two (4744) and S.S.A., Level Three (20074). SoundTrax CD available (20075).

geth-er for all time.___ Hand in hand,___ dreams com-bine,___

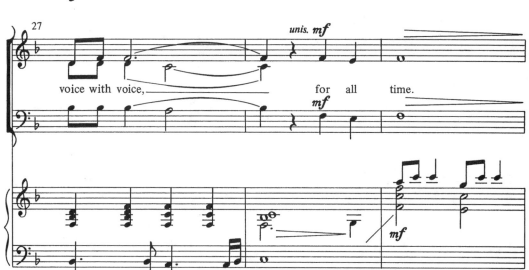

voice with voice,___ for all time.

I am a small part of the world. I have a

small voice ring-ing clear. But if I sing out for free-dom,—

and you

to - geth - er we have noth - ing left to

add your voice to mine,